A Blue Kiss, Sealed with The Keys

Abdul Fattah Ismail

Prologue

A kiss is a kiss
A smile is a smile

      A coat, filled in
blue
      Hers, filled with
red

The color of her favorite
Dancing out, then pulled
in sight

      His key, turned to
left
      Side then, tossed
      up into right

That Kind of Girl

The Who

The What

                       That Way?

The When

                       That Kind?

The Where

                       Those Legs?

The How

                       These Eyes?

The Why

                       Them Lips

The Who

                       Licked and Locked?

The What

                       The Look?

The When

                       A Laugh?

The Where

                       A Lowkey Smile From
Your Private Part?

The How

The Why

                       This is Who

With Whom?

                       This Could Be

Which One?

                       Know When is When

Feel It Wherever	That's How
Touch That How	That's How
See This Why	

Double Six

Just for awhile

Better yet, for as long as possible

I want to know those feelings

The feelings that came from waking up and kissing your
cheek

But no tongue is necessary then

Your index fingers grazing behind my ear, starts the
loving chill

That melts into a warm, expansive vapor

Running in dreams, then caught with life

Sí, vivimos la vida enamorada para que besamos los labios.

We must walk on the wild side at first, then run until our heels ache

When that happens, then let's climb onto the tree stump and sit down

We'll crunch on pears and mangoes from the market at the bottom of the hill

The one with clerks that works us with jaundiced eyes

¿Vale la peña?

Déjanos trabajarlo

Blue Measuring Tape

Distance between me and you

Would be zero if we were interested

In becoming untangled from our fears

Not so much interested, but capable

Because the capacity for the growth of imagination

Must exist for the value of interest to be coded before being defined

Then, and only then, is it examined and embraced with mutuality

Clear as fingernails

Better yet, if someone before me

Had given you the chance to pour out your heart

Into the passion of holding your red claw

Between the line creases; brown inside of your palm

If your family had told you that your drawings were colorful

If you felt the ray of sun from your bedroom window

Before brushing your teeth before school

If your mother was getting 63 cents more to match

The dollar of her colleague, who works less, plays more, and looks pale

If your father was allowed to steer his instincts

Away from the impulse of seeking entitlement

That looks true, but feels false

If your teachers taught you to explore the way

Your footprints can catch up to the gifts in the forest of your purpose

Defined by your genealogy

Smelled in the scent of that butter

Chillin out on your nails	Needing your ice
On your tonsils	Lying beneath your words
Which would be great to explore	
	Searching for your spice
After we take a walk from the café on Spuistraat	I sense it
	I am stimulated by it
My lips caress your own	But I know that I cannot have it

That's not my duty

I am not designed by the
earth to do that

Not because I am not
capable

But because that is not
important to you

When you think of me
more than once

In your department
meeting

I dream that you want to
feel

That I can hold you in the
desert

When the wind stills

As the dune covers our
eyesight

When we crawl on its
granules and grains

To the pier, then on a
boat where the blue
ocean massages our
eyelids

After the plane ride to
Beirut

Before zigging in the
crowded alleyways of
Prenzlauer Berg

Tight enough to make
your goosebumps notice

Soft enough to have
them dream with us

Single Birthdays On The Town, Single Valentines With The Glass

The pen is mightier than the sword

The one with a sharp blade and smooth, leather handle

The sword which can cut the heart

That deserts the foe from which the blade pierces the skin

The sword that moves with the passion

In the blood of the skin and bones that you are in

Bone marrow in the skeleton

Blood; rich with magenta in the dermis

Dancing beneath the epidermis

Pulsating at the flutter of your eyelash

After your lips caress each other

Writing the brief of Night Court

Inside the chamber

Beats by the ton

Barnard College

In good ole Indiana, I hit
from downtown on the
court

Once in awhile

In DC, I was a multiple
All-Star

But the nation's capital
started to finance

A priceless adjunct
fellowship

The first term had a
German mandate

We dominated the tennis
circuit, four years
straight

While you sprechen
deutsche

You taught me
generosity, sacrifice, and
diligence

Bitte Schoen

Before retirement, I
cultivated a bonzai
garden with seeds of
art, soul duets, and
technology

In two years, it sprouted
wisdom, motivation, and
elegance

Arigato

The garden was blown
away by steely
Honduran winds

Cut with sunny, spiritual
Tuesdays

Eight months of
consistency paved a trail
for railways

Gracias

Those cabooses hid for
comfy Korean cirrus
clouds

They glowed with grace
and empathy

Nine months of clear
days then turned into a
heavy downpour

Soon after, a higher
village beamed

Komawo

Six years stitched for a
doctorate in
romancology

Good for conquering
patriarchal society

Thank you, feminologists!

Possible to Connect

It is possible to

be a guy who loves

women as the heart

of society but thirsts for the

connection of one

amazing spirit

that can ride or die?

One that needs a whisper of support before a kiss by the
ear?

Then another million on the lips

and thousand on the shoulder?

Where we duck the

douches, the petty, the

brainwashed, the sheltered?

Is it possible to talk about our thoughts and test our
positions on everything? In the mental and physical?

The age of thirtysomething is asking for the heart.

Then we fly above the clouds, above the clouds where
the sounds are original

Is it?

Hell yeah, it is.

So hit me up.

Miss Brown

Love is all we need

Love is all I want

Hugs always feel good

Drugs sometimes make me feel great

Thugs are just pissed that they

        hate jazz because

        they're not cool enough

        to relate with that

        lovely vibration of tone

I never loved Lugz boots because they

                looked ugly to me

I never loved going to that church

        because everyone was old

        and white

Nowadays, I wonder if I can be loved

        like Bob Marley asked

Sometimes, nowadays, I can't wait to love

           someone again

Who it be?

When can we love for do?

Toss, then Drain

Love is something that I may have had before

But not from anyone right now

No, not like that

Like this zest of lemon; shaved

Like when you chop the peppers and zucchini plus tomatoes

Before boiling the water with oil and salt

After you shred two piles of Romano

When within that time, the black pepper grinder got filled

Once that happens, you look at the pasta jars

Of ziti, manicotti, ditalini, rotini, or penne on your counter

Triggering that moment when her cheeks beamed after the pappardelle at tré

You imagine a substitute grain doing the same

A perk from her cheeks could open her eyes wide, you think

You feel that it's only the pappardelle, so you go to the bodega

Warehouse of Loops

Foreigner. A mothafucking foreigner.

Wants to know what love is

He wants you to show us

As if that is your, better yet, my mothafucking problem

You see that I am tired, even though I took a long azz nap

Listen. But you cannot.

Or, you just don't know, cause you can't see.

It's finally all good.

Nah, for real.

I plan to walk away.

The adventure continues, to your video, through my radio

Blowing out your stereo

You know why? Because it goes like this....

In. Out. Out. In. Out. Out. Out. In. Out. In.

Audio sparked flints burning the bird in the hand

One less thing better than two in the bush

But worse without your fingers on my beard

Off it

Chick Forcefield

Just for awhile

Better yet, for as long as possible

I want to know those feelings

The feelings that come from waking up in the morning
and kissing your cheek

But no tongue. It ain't necessary then.

Your index fingers grazing behind my ear, starts the loving chill

That melts into a warm, expansive vapor

Knowing in dreams, then caught with life

Yea, viva la vida en el amor por tus hermosos labios

We must walk on the wild side at first, then run until our heels ache

When that happens, then let's climb onto the tree stump and sit there

We'll crunch on pears and mangoes from that market at the bottom of the hill

The one with clerks that mark us with jaundiced eyes

Seeing the bloom of our giggles after the lush whispers about this sunray on her arm

Grabbing your skin for life

Both eyes asking if we should turn down

For what? Please. Not you.

My Confessions

You may not have given it a thought

But that's okay

I was telling you the truth

In mysterious ways

Because I move in mysterious ways

I can't help it

As you know, we move around strongly

Speaking truth to power

I started to worry

That I had to be in the front

On the dial

So that you can tune in

You haven't tuned out, but why would you?

I need to pay tuition, then attention

To you, then me, then you

Once you speak

Then share a like

A Frosty

The snow warms your cheeks

After falling on dogwoods

Surrounded by deciduous trees

The snow invents playgrounds

Inviting young kids

Teaching cherubs rock and roll

The snow fights the passing of time

Losing in the end

Cause timing is everything

The snow dulls your windowsill

While brightening your spring fever

For days of romance, rain, and pollen

The snow blankets your eyelash

Slowing winks, but not stopping sight

Might as well make a snowman

Eyelash Academy

Pull up the wall, then brace your hips

So that your right leg catches up to your left one

Pull up on the boulder, then push your body

Over onto the ledge, with chest chlorophyll stains

Take advantage of that powder and green leaf

Filtered from your nails through your sciatic river

Voices only exist in blurry prints

Physical beauty exists in front of your eyelashes

Euphoria dances beyond the light shower

Stillborn revelations stay in it

Believe it or not, wisdom and euphoria have had an affair

That The New York Post missed on Page Six

If you want to know more about it

Don't ask US

Tell it to the people that don't climb boulders

They run around on the track in diagonals

Rated Z

You don't
connect with
me because it
is impossible
for you

You don't
relate to an
experience
with me that
can be
dignified

You don't
connect with
me because
your past
interactions
with my
gender

Have not
gone well

They have
been
poisoned by

actions fueled
with bile

You don't
connect with
me because
you don't feel
the need to
discover the
value of the
space
between us

Which is
minimal in
your mind

That is your
right;
inalienable,
invaluable

I am aware
of my
privilege

I am aware
that in order

to deconstruct
it, I must listen

Without
expectations

Of a
partnership
desired by
one, with
levels
undefined

Once we both
know this, I
will move on

Understandin
g that the
need for you
to love

Must go
through your
own journey

One where
preferences

of your own
heart

And ambitions
decide

Even society's
prescribed
laws mixed
with
geneticisms

Demand that I
chase you
within reason

With clever
plotting

Conducting
with sticks of
innuendo

After that pull
of indoe

6 puffs
before the
pass, 6
breaks from
your cheeks

Feeling that
our ability to
connect

Is just chance.
It meant
nothing.
Because we
live nowhere.

Peppered
with
circumstance.
As the axis
spins one
way.

You think that
you will find
the endpoint
of your road
to redemption

In the land of
nothing

Rather than
desire to
enter a brave
new world

Above this
netherworld

Where
everything is
a footprint to
hell

According to
everyone

Including the
voice from the
pain in your
elbow

Woken from
the flex of
your tricep

Harmony, felt
in our bones
at times, does
not exist

In an
environment
built for
deception

We know this

We march
against this
lie
perpetrated
as truth

In our systems.
In our cities. In
our
relationships

With solids,
liquids, and
gases

But we quit a
lot

Because the
days of pure
justice are a
long time ago

If they ever
existed

We imagine
because lies
are long

Past our
reproduction

Take 6

Beeswax

From one day

To the next

Texts jump from digital

To visceral

Punctuate with blended beans

Touched with honey love

Dipped by Portrait fingertips

Fine, smooth, clean

Purer than nectar

Blown by Cupid

Who doesn't lie

When you give it a try

Two hearts

Once beat

In the same room

Sometimes they stop

In both minds

Until then

Keep dreaming

Because it's too real

Bittersweet Chocolate Chips

My heart
cannot stop
the flutter

But my mind
shuddered to
think

My ears
heard your
urgency

My mind
danced in the
land of
confusion

My body
shook from
suburban
malaise

My
confidence
wavered from
blurred lines

Divided by
strangers

In an odd
bubble

An enclave
with slow
cognition

You took me
to the roof

The illusion
was warm

The cards slid
out even

The Players
Club popped

Then you
vanished

I wandered

Only because
you did

Then I sent an
e-card

Fireworks
popped

Then the
smoke rose in
the air

Then the
smoke
cleared

Then the fires
started

I held a
kerosene can

I dropped lit
matches from
my hot pocket

You tipped
the can

Every now
and then

Because you
like firemen

They do the
dirty work

They can take
the heat

They keep
their ass in
the kitchen

Of course
they do

You know
why?

I hired them

I'm Batman

I build to
connect by
day

I hang out at
night

Wearing a
silk
cummerbund
at 9 p.m.

Then a metal
chest plate at
1 a.m.

Strictly
business in the
mobile for
justice

Strictly
business for
the polity

It's risky
business

It's classy end
games

Untold, then
sold to your
fire chief

For a night on
the town
without you

And then her

I Love You, Mrs. Province

Do the math

Skate left, pivot right

Out the box

Pass the line

Step into millennium

Snap the foot

Lunge left, twist right

Slap the bark

Pushing clean aurelia

Throw a clothesline

Hung with cloth

Corner target

Lake splash

Passing gas

All dressed in nylon

Balloons, hot ass helium

You got a man down

Hand down

Bob the shoulder

North, south like Mark Jackson

The head wave

Checkmate

Zigzag Arrows

The elixir of lust

From the blue yonder

Rushing in

With blood to the head

Like an asteroid

You ask, don't stop

Don't stop the feeling

The feeling climaxes

To a hit

The feeling descends

Softly

Still carrying a big stick

Disintegrating into fine pixels

Of which a shadow is left

Peeking behind love

Where hope springs eternal

For that unconditional light

The Indifference Curve

Alone, alone, again,
again, or

Reach out

Together, together, for
once, for once

Alone, alone, again,
again, or

Together, again, for
once, for once

Or not this time

Sorry. Not personal.

But you're loud.

You talk a lot. You're
smart.

You're handsome. You're
cultured.

You're imaginative.
You're nice.

But you're broke. We
can be friends.

Maybe I'll see you
around. Maybe we'll get
together.

Probably not. Because a
desire ain't there.

For two to tango.

A deferred utility for the
deferred desire.
Sometimes.

The desire burns of love.
The deferment burns of
anxiety.

The disconnection cools
the spirit

To seal those gaps

Between them
fingerprints

To attach your senses

To my tone

Skin to skin

Lip to nape

From dusk to shadow

Through the still of grass
blades

Past the thrill in the dark

Wishing the present

Stays, then rests

Sitar Shakes

The eyes stroke the sunbeam pointing from above

Particles shift from invisible to tactile

Summoning a change through your frontal lobe

An ion in search of cations

Cations that run away from anions

Cations that run to other cations

Cations that pick up lost ions along the way

Burrowing a path inside your grey matter

Making it matter today and forever more

Until all the electromagnetic waves

Stream with the conduit of 20 strings

Swim along the contours of your hip valve

Sliver vocals from the soul, kissing your earlobe

To push your arms slowly into space

Unwound, unbothered

Reflexed, simulated

With all the grace

Without a trace

My Voice Over Prose to Call You

I just wanted to call

      and say that I love you

I just wanted to say how much

      I want to be there for you

I just wanted to say how much

      I want to be with you

To work for justice

      To build alliances

To run on beaches

      Playing tag

To rub oil on your shoulders and legs

      To jump off that pier on Annie's Place

Then run after the dead pirate ships on high tides in Mozambique

Before we march with the penguins of Simon's Town in the Cape

 Then swim with the guppies off of Banana Island in Sierra Leone

But who am I?

 To you, I can barely exist. To you, wondering if I am barely breathing

But my nostrils are built to flow routine waves, making Darth Vader laugh

 So laugh on.

Take this kiss and seal it.

Transit Jam

The love of life
 Slips up some

The love of life
 Stands up now

The love of life
　　　Swings a loop
　　　　　Like a quick flip

The love to love
　　　You and I

The love to love
　　　Grabs fresh fruit

The love to love
　　　Brows up high
　　　　　Winks in full gear

The trip of now
　　　Our first class

The trip of now
　　　Here in flesh

The trip of now
　　　At this pace
　　　　　Moves in that stride

Motions in our messaging massages the tensions to the past

Droplets

19 with Covid
Unknown
Unsure

Winter grey skies
No news
Good news

No girlfriend; Single
Alone
No work

20 with 20
Virus and Corona
Self and Quarantine

Together

Only the lonely
People with no sleep
Found
Before the lockdown

Bars closed
Restos closed
Bills late
No text back

Rent's due
Move it
Move it

Save breath
Save you

Spring Is Masked

New Moon Rising
Guiding
Slowly

Wildlife appears in towns and cities
Bisons stamp
Turtles stroll

Respect others
Set the growth of a red leaf
Feel the leaf after plucking the breath
Set inside of your palm

Pandemic swirls in
No kiss at night
In public
No touch

Then don't look back
Walk swiftly
Keep your mask on
Breathe slowly

....with no embrace

sure, it could have been great
       maybe, we could have been special
together, if we understand each other
       well, then it was the wrong time

or, we were not right for each other
       but, for me, I did not express my concerns
perhaps, this time in global shelter
       overthinking, will mean nothing

evolution, surfaces beyond the distant echo
       faded, into black, then now to yellow
beams, radiate from above into my mind and grey hairs
       impossible, means nothing when using time

meeting, the lover in her sleep

Unpeeled Thirst

Pick, pick, pick, pick
                Squirt swims over your nails
Outside before inside

                Deepening the joy
After the dig
                During the nibble

Nibbles open to press
                Firm, but smooth
With a sweep

                Cleared with a t-shirt
Wiped on my arm
                Pick, pick, pick

Juices flow with strength
                Tongues wired at ease
Body, better built for immunity

Vitamin C
                Put a smile on your face

Epilogue

To the keepers of the flame......

Look, but don't touch. Hold it within you.

CPSIA information can be obtained
at www.ICGtesting.com
Printed in the USA
BVHW091456170222
629333BV00015B/375